Famous
African Americans

LOUIS
ARMSTRONG

KING OF JAZZ

Patricia and
Fredrick McKissack

Enslow Elementary
an imprint of
Enslow Publishers, Inc.

40 Industrial Road
Box 398
Berkeley Heights, NJ 07922
USA

http://www.enslow.com

To Robert Carwell, Sr.
A special thanks to our friends at the
Missouri Historical Society in St. Louis

Enslow Elementary, an imprint of Enslow Publishers, Inc.

Enslow Elementary® is a registered trademark of Enslow Publishers, Inc.

Copyright © 2013 by Enslow Publishers, Inc.

All rights reserved.

Original edition published as *Louis Armstrong: Jazz Musician* in 1991.

Library of Congress Cataloging-in-Publication Data
    McKissack, Pat, 1944-
    Louis Armstrong : king of jazz / Patricia and Fredrick McKissack.
      p. cm. — (Famous African Americans)
    Includes bibliographical references and index.
    Summary: "A simple biography for early readers about Louis Armstrong's life"—Provided by publisher.
    ISBN 978-0-7660-4106-6
    1. Armstrong, Louis, 1901-1971—Juvenile literature. 2. Jazz musicians—United States—Biography—Juvenile literature. I. McKissack, Fredrick. II. Title.
    ML3930.A75M38 2013
    781.65092—dc23
    [B]

                         2012012302

Future editions
Paperback ISBN 978-1-4644-0200-5
ePUB ISBN 978-1-4645-1113-4
PDF ISBN 978-1-4646-1113-1

Printed in the United States of America

082012 Lake Book Manufacturing, Inc., Melrose Park, IL

10 9 8 7 6 5 4 3 2 1

To Our Readers: We have done our best to make sure all Internet Addresses in this book were active and appropriate when we went to press. However, the author and the publisher have no control over and assume no liability for the material available on those Internet sites or on other Web sites they may link to. Any comments or suggestions can be sent by e-mail to comments@enslow.com or to the address on the back cover.

Every effort has been made to locate all copyright holders of material used in this book. If any errors or omissions have occurred, corrections will be made in future editions of this book.

♻ Enslow Publishers, Inc., is committed to printing our books on recycled paper. The paper in every book contains 10% to 30% post-consumer waste (PCW). The cover board on the outside of each book contains 100% PCW. Our goal is to do our part to help young people and the environment too!

Photo Credits: AP Images, p. 20; Library of Congress, pp. 1, 3, 4, 14, 18; Louis Armstrong House & Archives at Queens College/CUNY, p. 10; Louisiana State Museum Jazz Collection, p. 13.

Illustration Credits: Ned O., pp. 7, 8, 16

Cover Photo: Library of Congress

Words in bold type are explained in *Words to Know* on page 22.

Series Consultant:
Russell Adams, PhD
Emeritus Professor
Afro-American Studies
Howard University

Contents

Louis Armstrong was a trumpeter and singer whose music changed the sound of jazz forever.

CHAPTER 1
OFF TO A BAD START

In 1900, New Orleans, Louisiana, was a busy city. One of the places people liked to go for a good time was Black Storyville.

Black Storyville had lots of bars and **dance halls**. There were lots of fights. Louis Armstrong was born in Storyville on August 4, 1901.

Louis's family was very poor. His mother, Mayann, did different jobs. Grandmama Josephine took care of Louis until he was five years old.

Then he went to live with his mother and his little sister, who was called Mama Lucy. Their home was a one-room shack. Louis's father was not around very much.

Black Storyville was full of crime. But something very special was happening there. A new kind of music was being played. It was called jazz.

Louis loved the sound of Storyville jazz. It was a part of him. No other music was like **jazz**. It was special.

Grandmama Josephine took Louis to church almost every Sunday. Louis enjoyed singing the old **spirituals**. Those old songs were special to him, too.

Louis often skipped school. Instead he sold newspapers on the street. He used the money to help buy food for his family. He dropped out of school when he was eleven.

"You're going to end up in trouble," Grandmama Josephine always warned Louis. And she was right.

As a young boy, Louis enjoyed music. He liked to sing in church with his grandmother.

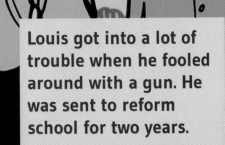

Louis got into a lot of trouble when he fooled around with a gun. He was sent to reform school for two years.

CHAPTER 2
IN TROUBLE

. . . .

Louis and three of his friends started a singing group. They sang on street corners for money.

One day Louis found a gun in an old trunk. He waited until New Year's Eve. He wanted to greet the New Year with loud gunshots. On the street, a boy fired a small gun. Then Louis shot his gun. His friends laughed and cheered. He pointed the gun into the air . . . and pulled the trigger.

Suddenly a policeman took hold of Louis.

The bullets were not real. No one was really hurt. Louis was just trying to have fun.

But the **judge** didn't see it that way. Louis broke the law. He was sent to **reform school**.

Louis was twelve years old. "I thought the world was coming to an end," he said later.

Louis was sent to reform school at the Colored Waifs' Home for Boys. There he joined the brass band.

Peter Davis taught music at the school. He asked Louis to play the **cornet**. Louis joined the **brass band**. By the end of the year, he was leading the band.

Once Louis led the band through Storyville. His family cheered. So did his friends. It was a day Louis never forgot.

Louis stayed in reform school for about two years. "Being there saved my life," he said years later.

CHAPTER 3
AND ALL THAT JAZZ

Louis was sent to live with his father. But before long, he was back with his mother in Black Storyville.

He took a job driving a cart full of coal. With his money, he bought an old horn. He started playing with jazz bands in Storyville bars. He worked all day and played his horn at night.

In 1917 many black jazz **musicians** went to Chicago and New York to play. One great trumpeter was Joe Oliver. He liked Louis. Louis thought Oliver was the best **trumpeter**.

When Oliver left for Chicago, Louis was asked to take his seat in the Kid Ory Band. At last Louis got a chance to be heard.

Soon people were coming to Black Storyville just to hear Louis Armstrong.

As a teenager, one of Louis's jobs was playing in a band (third from right) on a riverboat. He also washed dishes on the boat.

In the 1920s, more and more people began listening to jazz. Louis became a very popular musician.

Joe Oliver asked Louis to come play the cornet in Chicago. So he went. There he married Lil Hardin. She played the piano.

Lil wanted Louis to start his own band. But Louis wasn't ready. He played with some of the best bands in New York and Chicago.

In the 1920s, everyone was talking about jazz . . . jazz . . . and more jazz. And the jazz player most people were talking about was Louis Armstrong.

Louis started singing as well as playing trumpet. His voice had a very different sound.

CHAPTER 4
OH, YEAAAAAH!

· ·

For many years Louis played the cornet. One night he played the **trumpet**. It was larger than the cornet. He liked its sound. From then on he played the trumpet.

Louis also made records with many different bands. More and more people heard his music. He made them love the sounds of Storyville jazz the same way he did. "It's a hot sound," he said. Then he would wipe his face with a big, white handkerchief.

At last Louis started his own band. They went all over the United States playing jazz . . . jazz . . . and more jazz.

Sometimes when Louis played he also sang. His voice sounded like he had a bad cold. But that was his own special sound.

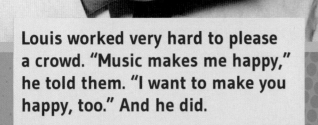

There is a story people tell about Louis Armstrong. It may or may not be true. It is said that one night he was singing and forgot the words. So he made trumpet sounds with his voice. Do-skid-dat-de-dat-dat-do. That way of singing is called **scatting**.

And at the end of a song, Louis always sang, "Oh, yeaaaaah!" People waited so that they could join him in singing, "Oh, yeaaaaah!"

Louis worked very hard to please a crowd. "Music makes me happy," he told them. "I want to make you happy, too." And he did.

CHAPTER 5
SATCHMO

. . . .

Louis had not taken his band to New Orleans. So in 1931 he went back to his home city.

His mother, Mayann, had died in 1927. But the rest of his family came to hear his band play.

Some people in the South thought black and white musicians should not play together in the same band. Louis thought differently. His band had members of different races. So Louis and his band were turned away from some hotels.

They were called names. But his band stayed together and played great music. Lots of people came to hear them, and they enjoyed the music.

Louis Armstrong's unique style of music still brings joy to many people today.

Louis's friends called him "Satchel Mouth" because his smile was so big. (A satchel is a suitcase that opens wide.) Over the years, "Satchel Mouth" became "Satchmo." By the late 1930s, everybody was calling Louis "Satchmo." And he loved it.

Louis and Lil were no longer together. There were always large crowds around him. But Satchmo was lonely. His music was sad. Then he married Lucille Wilson, a beautiful dancer. Satchmo was happy again. So was his music.

In 1960, Louis Armstrong was named a **goodwill ambassador.** He went all over the world playing music and making friends.

Satchmo made many records. He was in several movies. He had one big hit song: "Hello, Dolly!" It sold millions of copies. He also won many **awards**. He never wanted to stop playing music.

And he never did. He lived and made music until he was almost seventy years old.

He died on July 6, 1971.

WORDS TO KNOW

award—An honor given to a person who has done something special.

brass band—A group of musicians who play the brass horns: trombone, tuba, French horn, trumpet, or cornet.

cornet—A brass horn; a musical instrument.

dance hall—A place where people go to dance.

goodwill ambassador—A person who represents the United States around the world.

jazz—A special type of music developed in the early 1900s.

judge—The person who decides a court case.

musicians—People who play instruments and make music.

reform school—A special school where children who get into trouble with the law are sent.

scatting—A kind of singing without using words. A person's voice is used to make sounds like an instrument.

spirituals—Religious songs that were first sung by African-American slaves.

trumpet—A brass horn; a musical instrument.

trumpeter—A person who plays the trumpet.

LEARN MORE

BOOKS

Elish, Dan. *Louis Armstrong and the Jazz Age.* New York: Children's Press, 2008.

Kimmel, Eric A. *A Horn for Louis.* New York: Random House, 2006.

Raum, Elizabeth. *Louis Armstrong.* Mankato, Minn.: Capstone Press, 2006.

WEB SITES

Jazz Kids: Now and Then
<http://www.pbs.org/jazz/kids/nowthen/louis.html>

Louis Armstrong Discography
<http://www.satchography.com>

INDEX